VEG

30 Days of Vegan Recipes and Meal Plans for Increasing Your Health and Energy

REMEMBER TO JOIN THE GROUP NOW!

If you have not joined the Mastermind Self Development group yet, now is your time! You will receive videos and articles from top authorities in self development as well as a special group only offers on new books and training programs. There will also be a monthly member only draw that gives you a chance to win any book from your Kindle wish list!

If you sign up through this link http://www.mastermindselfdevelopment.com/specialreport you will also get a special free report on the Wheel of Life. This report will give you a visual look at your current life and then take you through a series of exercises that will help you plan what your perfect life looks like. The workbook does not end there; we then take you through a process to help you plan how to achieve that perfect life. The process is very powerful and has the potential to change your life forever. Join the group now and start to change your life! http://www.mastermindselfdevelopment.com/specialreport

Introduction

Veganism is fast catching up with many people across the world. The noble idea behind veganism, such as not wanting to exploit the less fortunate animal species of the world by taking what is theirs and selfishly using it for ourselves simply because they do not have the power to stop us, is perhaps, the primary reason for the growth in popularity of this concept.

However, in addition to the above extremely thoughtful reason, the health benefits and other great things about veganism are all sufficiently powerful causes for the expansion of the idea of veganism across the planet. This book is written with an intention to exhort newcomers to try a one-month vegan challenge that has the power to change not just your lifestyle but your entire outlook on life.

Before you decide to try to change your lifestyle to vegan, there are a few things you must know and understand about it. This book aims to do exactly that by giving you a detailed overview in the following areas:

- What is veganism?
- A brief history on veganism
- How is veganism useful to you?
- Meal plans for a one-month challenge

along with recipe outlines
- How to stay committed to the cause?

What is veganism?

You know who vegetarians are? They do not consume poultry, meat, or fish in their diet. Vegans, additionally, do not consume or use any animal products and/or by-products such as dairy products, honey, eggs, leather, silk, fur, and soaps and cosmetics made from animal sources. Vegans are the superset of vegetarians. All vegans are also vegetarians but all vegetarians need not be vegans.

Vegans believe that veganism is not just about their diet but a way of life. As far as possible, vegans avoid exploitation of animals in any form including but not limited to food, clothing, or other purposes. They also avoid items that have been tested on animals before being commercialized. And believe it or not, there is a vegan diet for all kinds of diets ranging from the junk food lovers to the raw food lovers and those in between, too.

History of Veganism

Veganism, although not known as veganism, has been around for many centuries. Examples of prevention of exploitation against and cruelty to animals have been written in history books. Lord Buddha of India and Pythagoras both advocated this concept and had put in rules to ensure their followers ate only plant-based food and completely avoided meats and animal products.

The earliest modern-day veganism is known to have occurred around 1806 CE. During that time, the great English poet P. B. Shelley and Dr. William Lambe publicly objected to consuming dairy products and eggs by humans on ethical grounds. This incident seems to have laid the foundation for modern-day veganism.

In November 1944, six non-dairy vegetarians including Donald Watson and Elsie Shrigley met together and discussed the topic on non-dairy vegetarians' lifestyles and diets. Despite strong opposition, these six members founded the new movement and became actively involved in this new project.

When the Vegan Society was formalized and registered as a charity organization in 1979, the Memorandum and Articles of Association of the society defined veganism as:

"...a philosophy and way of living which seeks to exclude – as far as possible and practicable – all forms of exploitation of, and cruelty to,

animals for food, clothing or any other purpose; and by extension, promotes the development and use of animal-free alternatives for the benefit of humans, animals, and the environment. In dietary terms, it denotes the practice of dispensing with all products derived wholly or partly from animals."

This book deals only with the dietary aspect of veganism, giving you ample sufficient reasons to shift your lifestyle to this healthy and noble one. While the benefits of turning vegan are discussed in another chapter, the kind of foods that you can include in your diet while keeping your energy levels and health not just unchanged but also improved than earlier is huge.

Here is a small list of foods that are known to be totally vegan:

- All kinds of grains and cereals
- All kinds of beans and legumes
- All fruits and vegetables

Other vegan foods include soy milk, vegan mayonnaise, vegan ice cream and cheese, vegan hot dogs, and more. Moreover, a lot of companies have come out with mock meats that give vegans a sense of eating meat. This book also has four chapters dedicated to making vegan foods, which includes easy-to-make recipes.

Chapter 1: Why Go Vegan?

Most people in the world want to do the following things by some means or the other:

- Lose weight
- Eat better
- Get fitter and healthier
- Do something for society and the world at large

The great news is that if you shift to a vegan diet, you can achieve all the above goals. And let me assure you, you will enjoy delicious, wholesome, and satiating meals as well.

No loss or reduction in energy levels – There is a misconception that changing to a vegan diet reduces your energy levels. There are numerous unworthy talks of vegans living only on water and a few greens and hence their energy levels have taken a huge dip. And on the other side of the spectrum, there are plenty of spurious rumors that say going vegan is helping them do impossible things. These other-end-of-the-spectrum talks make out vegans to be people who can walk on water! Let me assure you that neither of the extremes is true or based on any scientific studies.

Health benefits are huge when you choose to go vegan. Of course, the initial learning curve is going to be steep and you would have to counter multiple challenges. However, once you have overcome these tough phases and complete the 30-day challenge, you are going feel to happier, lighter, and more fit. Moreover, there are multiple studies done by various organizations including the British Dietetic Association that has proven the excellent efficacies of getting fitter and healthier by following a vegan diet.

Here is the list of a few magic foods that can restore energy instantaneously:

Bananas – Already beautifully and naturally packaged by nature, this wonderful tropical fruit is normally the first you must reach out for when you feel tired or fatigued.

Walnuts – Another great pick-me-up tree nut, walnuts are rich in plant proteins, omega fatty acids, and vitamins giving you the almost-instant energy boost.

Green smoothies – Delicious smoothies made by tossing together strawberries, bananas, and orange juices are great and extremely healthy pick-me-ups to fight fatigue.

Coconut water – This is nature's energy drink

and is amazingly refreshing and is filled with vitamins and potassium.

Kiwi – This low-fat delicious fruit is an instant energy enhancer triggered by the simple sugars present in it.

Why I chose to mention vegan energy boosters in the beginning itself is to help you overcome doubts regarding your ability to get on with your daily schedule if you choose to go vegan. Today there are many sportspeople who have shifted to this diet to keep fitter and sustain energy levels. So, if highly active people in the field of sports can take advantage of veganism, it should not be difficult for moderately active people like us to take this 30-day challenge and come out with flying colors.

Other great reasons to take the one-month challenge to go vegan are:

Lose weight and yet remain energized – Many of us would love to find a sensible way to lose excess weight and yet remain healthy and fit. Average vegans are known to weigh 20 pounds lesser than average meat-eaters. Despite this, vegan diets do not starve you and make you feel enervated like the usual run-of-the-meal fad diets do.

Keep diseases and health disorders away – The Academy of Nutrition and Dietetics have conducted multiple studies which show that taking the vegan route helps you steer clear of common disorders such as diabetes, hypertension or high blood pressure thereby preventing the onset of many modern-day diseases such as heart attacks, kidney failure, and others.

Vegan foods are yummy and delicious – If you thought going vegan means you would have to give up your favorite ice creams, hamburgers, and chicken sandwiches, then you are wrong. With demand for vegan products soaring, many companies are coming up with amazingly delicious vegan options that taste very much like the non-vegetarian stuff. You will not miss any of the meats and animal products at all. There are plenty of established brands that cater to veganism and deliver really tasty dairy and meat substitutes.

Vegan diets are full of highly nutritious and healthy food items including whole grains, beans and legumes, nuts, soy products, and fresh fruits and vegetables. Here are some of the health benefits that these fiber-rich and healthy food sources provide you with:

- **Minimal saturated fats** – Meats and

dairy products contain plenty of saturated fats thereby increasing the risk of cardiovascular diseases. Vegan diets automatically reduce intake of saturated fats enhancing your health condition

- **Fiber** – A vegan diet is high in fiber content that is very conducive to healthy bowel movements.

- **Magnesium** – Dark, green leafy vegetables are a rich source of magnesium, a key element that aids the body in the absorption of calcium.

- **Potassium** – Similarly, potassium, an important mineral that balances acidity and water in our body and helps in the removal of toxins, is found plenty in plant-based foods.

- **Proteins** – Meat-eaters invariably end up with more proteins than is needed by the body. Vegan diets, which include nuts, beans, and legumes, have the right amount of proteins for us.

Vegan diets provide other critically essential nutrients such as Vitamins E and C, phytochemicals, antioxidants, and foliates. These help in keeping your immunity system healthy and robust, and also prevent age-related diseases such as Alzheimer's and Parkinson's disease and keep your overall body organs functioning well.

Vegan diets have the power to prevent the following diseases that are very common in today's high-stress unhealthy lifestyle:

- Cardiovascular diseases
- Reduced cholesterol due to the complete absence of meat and dairy products in your diet
- Age-related macular degeneration
- Reduced risk of breast cancer
- Reduced risk of contracting ailments like diabetes, hypertension, cataracts, colon and prostate cancer, arthritis, and osteoporosis

In addition to improved health and prevention of diseases, going vegan makes you stronger, more energetic, and more attractive. Here is how:

Lowered Body Mass Index – Cutting meat and dairy out of your diet naturally reduces Body Mass Index.

Weight loss – Weight loss is an unquestioned effect of a vegan diet.

Healthy skin – Consuming rich sources of

Vitamins A and E from nuts and fruits and vegetables enhance the texture and health of your skin.

Reduced allergy symptoms – Plant-based foods do not trigger as many allergic reactions in humans as dairy and meat products do.

Less intake of mercury – A lot of shellfish and fish contain high levels of mercury, which we take in when we eat these foods. Switching to veganism does away with this toxin completely.

The above are only some of the great reasons that you must start off this 30-day vegan challenge. Instead of finding reasons not to do something good, focus on the above reasons which tell you why you should do it and dive straight in. Summon some extra willpower and after you complete this challenge you can rest assured that the willpower would come on its own when you see and feel the wondrous new VEGAN YOU.

Chapter 2: Understanding Vegan Diets

In the previous chapter, along with why should you go vegan, I had mentioned some basic foods that can deliver instant energy whenever you feel enervated. Just to reiterate, the foods listed are all completely vegan and yet are employed by all to get back energy levels when they feel sapped.

Considering the many misconceptions, doubts, and skepticism regarding energy levels and maintenance of good health by vegans, I thought it made sense to dedicate one chapter to help you overcome these misunderstandings which in turn will, I hope, catapult your move to try out the 30-day vegan challenge.

There are many ex-vegans who complain of fogginess, depression, and other challenging mental and social circumstances when they choose to give up animal foods. Understanding the power and function of each nutrient is very helpful in managing those seemingly difficult days, especially during the initial adjustment phase of this diet.

Knowing how the various nutrients derived from animal and plant sources differ from each other, which vegan foods give you optimum results, and how to keep feelings of depression at bay due to short-term failures, are all critical elements in making a success of your 30-day vegan challenge. And when you come out successful in a small attempt, you will be emboldened to try for something bigger.

Carbohydrates for vegans – Cutting back on carbohydrates is not that difficult for anyone, including us vegans. It is essential for you to use low-carb food sources to maintain good health with a vegan diet.

Vegetables: There are many vegetables which are low-carb foods including onions, tomatoes, eggplant, cauliflower, broccoli, bell peppers, and more.

Fruits: Blueberries and strawberries are low-carb foods. However, depending on how much you need daily, other fruits can easily be included.

Fatty foods – Olives and avocados are high in good fats and are low-carb too, hence they are excellent dietary inclusions for vegans.

Soy, nuts, and seeds: These are low in carbohydrates and high in fats and proteins. So, it is imperative to include soy, soy-based foods, nuts, and seeds into your daily diet.

Chia seeds: I deliberately included this one special item because most of the carbohydrates in chia seeds are in the form of fiber. Hence, most of the energy source from this food comes from fats and proteins. Do include chia seeds whenever you can.

Additionally, choose slow carbohydrate foods, that is, consume carb sources that have a low glycemic index. These foods prevent high fluctuations in your blood sugar levels and you will feel more satiated over a longer period as they release glucose slowly. For instance, choose breads that have been made from non-ground grains, use barley, quinoa, and oats in place of rice, use fresh beans and legumes instead of canned ones, use sweet potatoes instead of white potatoes.

Animal Protein Vs. Plant Protein – As our body does not accumulate protein, it is imperative that we take in proteins in our daily diet. Proteins are available both in plant-based and animal-based foods. The difference between the two sources is the profile of amino acids present. Amino acids are of different types (about twenty of them are very critical for us) and all of them are essential for carrying out multiple metabolic activities in our body.

Animal proteins invariably have a sufficiently wide range of amino acids in them whereas many plant proteins are not complete. For instance, many plant proteins are quite low in important amino acids such as tryptophan, methionine, isoleucine, and lysine. Legumes, on the other hand, are the best plant-based protein source that is comparable to meats. For this express reason, ensure you eat 3 servings of legumes daily in the form of peas, beans, peanuts, tofu, etc. This will keep your energy levels optimum and considerably reduce your craving for meats.

Fats in vegan diets – Very low-fat foods are not great for vegan diets. In fact, a lot of recent studies have proved that very low-fat diets are not effective in the long-term. However, a free-for-all fatty diet is also an absolute no-no. It is important to include good-fat foods such as nuts and avocados to get the right quality and quantity of fat. Nutrition experts believe you should consume not more than 30 gm. of saturated fats every day.

Vitamins, Omega-3 fats, and other important nutrients – Animal protein foods contain higher levels and a wider range of other important nutrients such as Vitamins (B12 and D), DHA (Docosahexaenoic acid), which is an essential omega-3 fatty acid, zinc, and heme iron. The four listed nutrients are found in abundance in meats such as pork, beef, dairy products, eggs, and fish, but are a little low in plant-based foods.

While this may seem a concern, let me assure you that there are ample solutions for this, other than simply giving up a fantastically healthy lifestyle, that have the power to change multiple things in a positive way (already discussed in the previous chapter). Omega-3 fatty acids are available in plenty in walnuts, flaxseed and flaxseed oil, and chia seeds. Vitamin B12 plant-based analogs include sourdough bread, fermented soy foods, shiitake mushrooms, and sea vegetables. Moreover, these trace nutritional elements like Vitamin B12, Vitamin D, iodine etc. can be easily taken as supplements.

Most plant-based foods are rich in folate (dark, green leafy veggies provide this nutrient in plenty), potassium, calcium (figs, nuts, almonds etc. are wonderfully rich in calcium), iron (lentils are a great source) Vitamin C, phytochemicals, and Vitamin A (carrots). So these nutrients are well covered in a vegan diet through the intake of ample amounts of differently colored fruits and vegetables.

Do not hesitate to use convenience foods
– There are plenty of convenience products for vegans available in the market today. These include vegan ice creams, vegan meats, and vegan cheeses. When you are pressed for time and need convenience over laborious cooking processes, do not hesitate to use these options as they will go a long way in helping you stay committed to the vegan cause, especially in the early days when you are in the learning curve.

Chapter 3: Meal Plan and Outline Recipes for Block I

The next few chapters are dedicated to giving you meal plans along with some basic recipes and motivation for the start of your 30-day vegan challenge journey.

Day 1

"The secret of getting ahead is getting started."

- *Mark Twain*

Green smoothies for Breakfast

What to use:
- Mango juice (1/4 cup)
- Coconut Water (1/2 cup)
- Parsley (1/2 cup, fresh)
- Cilantro (1/2 cup, fresh) -coriander
- Avocado (1/2 – 1)
- Ice

What to do:
In a blender, mix mango juice and coconut water until the two are smoothly blended. Now add parsley, cilantro, avocado, and ice cubes and blend again to get a thick, super smooth smoothie. Adjust tartness and sweetness levels

with sweetener choice to match your liking.

Lemon and Citrus Couscous with Fennel and Chickpeas for Lunch

What to use:
- Fennel (1 cup, trimmed)
- Chickpeas (2 cups, cooked)
- Coriander (1/4 cup)
- Couscous (3 cups)
- Lemon Juice (1 tbsp.)
- Kalamata Olives (1/3 cup)
- Orange Juice (1/3 cup)
- Citrus zest (1 ½ tbsp.)
- Olive oil (3 tbsp.)

What to do:
In a pan, cook the trimmed fennel until it reaches caramelization. To this, add cooked chickpeas, ground coriander, lemon juice, and kalamata olives and continue cooking over a medium flame until you have a nice veggie-filled sauce. To give the couscous a citrusy flavor, cook it in a mixture of orange juice and water along with some lemon and orange zest, a little olive oil, and salt. To serve this couscous meal, fluff up the couscous using a fork. Make a layer of the couscous plate and over it, spoon out the fennel and chickpeas mixture. You can now use the fennel frond for garnishing. Dig into your delicious vegan lunch.

Tofu-Spinach Lasagna for Dinner -

What to Use:
- Lasagna noodles (24 oz.)
- Spinach (12 oz., frozen, chopped)
- Tofu (12 oz.)
- Sugar (1/4 tsp.)
- Soymilk (1/4 cup)
- Lemon Juice (1 tbsp.)
- Garlic powder (1 tsp.)
- Salt (1/2 tsp.)
- Basil (1 cup)
- Tomato Sauce (1 ½ cups)

What to do:
Cook the lasagna noodles as directed on the package, drain and keep aside. Squeeze the spinach to remove water as much as possible. In a blender, blitz together sugar, tofu, soymilk, lemon juice, garlic powder, salt, and basil until you get a smooth blend. Now, stir in the dried spinach. Take a baking dish and make a layer of tomato sauce at the bottom. Make a layer of the cooked lasagna noodles over this and over this a layer of the tofu mixture. Repeat the three layers again until all the materials are used up. The top layer should be that of the noodles and tomato sauce poured over it. In a preheated oven, bake this for about 25-30 minutes. Enjoy.

Day 2

Mango Smoothie for Breakfast -

What to use:
- Mango (frozen, 2 cups)
- Orange juice (1 ½ cups)
- Lime zest (½ tsp.)
- Maple syrup (pure)
- Avocado (1/2 cup)

What to do:
Add 2 cups frozen mango, 1 ½ cup orange juice, ½ cup avocado, ½ tsp lime zest, pure maple syrup (to taste), and appropriate amount of water into a blender and blitz together everything until you get a lovely, thick, and creamy smoothie.

Avocado and sauerkraut sandwiches for lunch -

What to Use:

- Dijon mustard (to taste)
- Bread (pumpernickel or rye)
- Vegan Thousand Island dressing (to taste)
- Sauerkraut (2 oz.)
- Avocado (1/2)

What to do:
Spread Dijon mustard on one slice of pumpernickel or rye bread and spread Thousand Island vegan dressing on the other slice. On an oiled (lightly) skillet, place the two slices (dry side down) and grill until golden brown. Pile on sauerkraut topping for one slice and avocado on the other slice. Continue to grill over medium heat for about 5 minutes. Remove from heat and join two halves and enjoy. Combine with cucumber and tomato salad for a complete vegan meal.

Scallion Pancakes for Dinner -

What to use:
- All-purpose flour (2 cups)
- Vegetable shortening (2 tsp.)
- Salt (1/2 tsp.)
- Green Onions (1/2 cup)
- Oil (1/4 cup)

What to do:
Make pancake dough with all-purpose flour,

knead well and keep aside for some time. Then roll out the dough (1/8-inch thickness); spread a layer of vegetable shortening, and then sprinkle a layer of salt and then a layer of green onions. Gently roll this into a jelly-shaped roll and cut out fist-sized pieces. Again, with rolling pin, roll out each piece into 1/8-inch thick slices and cook on an oiled skillet for about 2 minutes each, or until golden brown. Place the cooked pancakes on paper tissues to remove the excess oil and dig in. You could use soy sauce as a tartar dip.

Day 3

"If you're happy, if you're feeling good, then nothing else matters."

- *Robin Wright*

Chocolate Hemp Smoothie for Breakfast

–

What to use:
- Almond Milk (2 cups)
- Pitted Dates (1/3 cup)
- Unsweetened cocoa powder (3 tbsp.)
- Hemp seeds (3 tbsp.)
- Banana (1, whole)
- Cinnamon (¼ tsp.)
- Ice

What to do:
In a blender add almond milk (2 cups), 1/3 cup pitted dates, 3 tbsp. unsweetened cocoa powder, 3 tbsp. hemp seeds (hulled), 1 banana (peeled and cut into slices/cubes), ¼ tsp cinnamon powder, and ice cubes. Blend it all together until the mixture reaches a thick, creamy, and smoothie-like (though this will be of a slightly thinner consistency) consistency. Pour into a glass and drink away.

Minestrone Soup and Crusty Bread for Lunch –

What to use:
- Olive oil (1 tbsp.)
- Onions (¾ cup, chopped)
- Zucchini (1/2 diced)
- Carrots (2, chopped)
- Beans (3 cups)
- Tomatoes (1 diced)
- Garlic (1 clove, minced)
- Celery (2 stalks, diced)
- Basil (1/4 cup)
- Pepper (1 tsp.)
- Salt (2/3 tsp.)
- Oregano (1 tsp.)
- Water (6 cups)
- Macaroni noodles (2 cups)

What to do:
In a saucepan, heat 1 tbsp. of olive oil (extra virgin) over medium heat. Sauté ¾ cup finely chopped onions, and add the following: water, diced zucchini, carrots, beans, diced tomatoes, minced garlic, diced celery, dried basil, and pepper, oregano, and salt. Bring all this to a boil, and simmer for about 25-30 minutes until all ingredients are cooked. Now add macaroni and cook for another 10 minutes. Adjust spices to your taste and serve hot with some

pumpernickel or rye bread (roasted on a skillet with a dash of oil).

Vegan sausages for dinner -

What to use:
- Beans (2 cups, personal choice for base)
- Olive oil (2 tsp.)
- Soy sauce (2 tbsp.)
- Garlic (1 clove, minced)
- Wheat gluten (1 tsp.)
- Yeast (1 tsp.)
- Fennel seeds (1/3 cup, crushed)
- Red pepper flakes (1/2 tbsp.)
- Pepper (1 tsp.)
- Oregano (1 tsp.)
- Salt (1 tbsp.)

What to do:
Get your steaming apparatus ready with water brought to a full boil. Cool and mash your chosen beans for a base nicely until no lumps are left. Add olive oil, soy sauce, finely minced garlic, wheat gluten, nutritional yeast, crushed fennel seeds, red pepper flakes, pepper, oregano, and salt and mix well until you get nice smooth dough-like consistency. Divide this dough into 4-6 portions and make each portion into a log shape (like the meat sausages). Place these on separate tin foils and roll the foil to look like a tootsie roll. Put these wrapped vegan

sausages in the steamer and cook for about 40 minutes. Remove from heat and your vegan sausages are ready. Serve hot with a nice soy sauce dip or simply with ketchup.

Day 4

"Veganism is not a sacrifice. It is a joy."

  -   *Gary L. Francion*

Peanut Butter Banana Smoothie for Breakfast –

What to use:
- Bananas (2 whole, frozen)
- Dates (4 whole)
- Peanut butter (1 tbsp.)
- Chia seeds (1 tbsp.)
- Water (¼ cup)

What to do:
In a blender, add 2 sliced frozen bananas, 4 small dates, 1 tbsp. peanut butter, 1 tbsp. chia seeds, and ¼ cup water. Blitz together until well blended and your smoothie is ready.

Asparagus, Potato, and Squash Frittata for Lunch -

Ingredients:

Squash (1, sliced)
Potatoes (2 sliced)
Garlic (1 clove, minced)

Italian Herbs (1 tsp.)
Onion (1/2 onion)
Salt (1 tsp.)
Pepper (2 tbsp.)
Asparagus (12 oz.)
Tofu (8 oz.)

Fry the squash and potatoes until golden brown. Next, add garlic, dried herbs, and onions and continue to sauté until the onions are soft. Add salt and pepper for seasoning. Now, put in the asparagus and stir over heat for a couple more minutes. Put this veggie mixture into cake tin. In a blender, blitz together tofu and other remaining ingredients (except the dried herbs) until smooth. Now add the herbs and mix well. Pour this tofu mixture onto the veggie layer. Smoothen out the tofu layer with a knife and bake for 30-40 minutes in a medium heat oven.

Tempeh Casserole for Dinner -

What to use:
- Tempeh (8 oz.)
- Onions (1 diced)
- Zucchini (1 sliced)
- Broccoli stock (2 cups)
- Brown rice (2 cups)
- Arrowroot starch (1 tbsp.)
- Balsamic vinegar (3 tbsp.)

- Herbs (2 tbsp.)
- Baking powder (1 tbsp.)
- Egg Substitute (1/4 cup)
- Vegan mayo (3 tsp.)
- Paprika (1/2 tsp.)
- Salt (1/4 tsp.)

What to do:

Mash the tempeh either in a food processor or with a potato masher. In a big bowl, mix this mashed tempeh with onions, zucchini, broccoli stock, brown rice, arrowroot starch, balsamic vinegar, herbs, baking powder, and egg substitute and place in a casserole dish. In a preheated oven at 350F, cook for about 20 minutes. For the sauce, combine vegan mayo, paprika, and salt. Serve hot.

Day 5

"As I improved my diet, I started to learn to love myself, probably for the first time ever."

- *Frank Ferrante*

Strawberry and Avocado Smoothie for Breakfast –

What to use:
- Banana (1/2 frozen)
- Strawberries (fresh, 2 cups)
- Spearmint (3 tbsp.)
- Coconut water (1 ½ cups)
- Avocado (1/2)
- Date (pitted)
- Ice

What to do:
In a food processor, blend together ½ a frozen banana, 2 cups of fresh strawberries, 3 tbsp. of spearmint, 1 ½ cups of coconut water, ½ an avocado, 1 pitted date, and ice cubes. Your smoothie is ready to drink.

Adzuki Bean Burgers with Potato Wedges for Lunch -

What to use:

- Oats (1 package, prepackaged)
- Olive oil (2 tbsp.)
- Celery (2 stalks, finely chopped)
- Onion (chopped)
- Garlic (1 clove)
- Carrots (2 chopped)
- Salt (1 tbsp.)
- Basil (3 tbsp.)
- Water (2 cups)
- Adzuki beans (1 cup)
- Parsley (2 tbsp.)
- Brown rice flour (1/4 cup)
- Bread (rye or pumpernickel)

What to do:

Boil the water in a saucepan and add a packet of oats. Simmer for about 2 minutes until the oats are cooked. Over a medium flame, heat 2 tbsp. of olive oil and put in celery, onions, garlic, and carrots and cook until tender. Add a little water, salt, and basil to this mixture and stir occasionally and cook for another 5 minutes.

In a food processor, blitz together the onion mixture, cooked oats, adzuki beans, and parsley. Stir in the brown rice flour until you get a dough-like consistency that can be molded into patties. Form 8-10 patties with this. Cook the patties on a skillet with a dash of oil. Place between toasted pumpernickel or rye bread and enjoy your meal.

Lentil and Barley Casserole for Dinner -

What to use:
- Oil (2 tbsp.)
- Onions (1 diced)
- Garlic (2 cloves, minced)
- Potatoes (3 diced)
- Swede (3 oz.)
- Carrots (3 chunked
- Rosemary (1 oz.)
- Bay leaves (1 oz.)
- Thyme (1 oz.)
- Tomato paste (1 cup)
- Water (5 cups)
- Pearl barley (2 oz.)
- Lentils (1/2 cup)
- Stock powder and cube (1 prepackaged)
- Mushrooms (2/3 cup)
- Pepper (1 tbsp.)

What to do:
In a large pan, heat oil and sauté the onions and garlic. Add potatoes, swede, and carrots (all cut into large chunks) and continue cooking until the veggies get tender. Put in rosemary, bay leaves, thyme, and tomato paste. Pour 5 cups of water and add pearl barley, lentils, stock powder, stock cube, and mushrooms. Add a little pepper for seasoning. Bring this mixture to a boil and then simmer over a low flame for

about 45 minutes until a casserole consistency is achieved. Remove the bay leaves and then serve.

Day 6

"It's not a diet. It's not a phase. It's a permanent lifestyle."

- *Anonymous*

Cherry limeade Smoothie for Breakfast
–

What to use:
- Peach (1 sliced)
- Cherries (frozen, 1 cup)
- Almond milk (¾ cup)
- Lime juice (1 lime, fresh squeezed)
- Ice

What to do:
In a blender, blend together 1 ripe peach (sliced), 1 cup frozen cherries, ¾ cup almond milk, juice of 1 lime, and some ice cubes. Your smoothie is ready.

Baked Potatoes and Coleslaw for Lunch
-

What to use:
- Olive oil (1 tbsp.)
- Potatoes (6 whole)
- Vegan cream cheese (3 oz.)

- Vegan mayo (4 tsp.)
- Mustard (3 tsp.)
- Cabbage (2 cups, chopped)
- Carrots (1 cup, chopped)
- Onions (2/3 cup, chopped)

What to do:
Smear a little olive oil on the washed and dried potatoes and bake in a preheated oven for about 1 to 1 ½ hours until soft on the inside and crisp on the outside. For the coleslaw, combine cream cheese, vegan mayonnaise, and mustard until you get a smooth mixture. Add this to finely chopped cabbage, carrots, and onions, and mix well. Season as needed and refrigerate. When the potatoes are ready, cut in the middle and add the coleslaw and serve.

Noodles with vegetables and tofu for dinner -

What you need:
- Soy sauce (4 tsp.)
- Sweet chili sauce (2 tsp.)
- Mushroom sauce (2 tsp.)
- Noodles (24 oz.)
- olive oil (1 tsp.)
- Onions (1/2, chopped)
- Ginger (1 oz. grated)
- Garlic (1 clove, minced)
- Vegetables of choice

- Tofu (12 oz.)

What to do:
In a small bowl, mix together soy sauce, sweet chili sauce, and vegetarian mushroom sauce. In a large bowl, put a packet of noodles and cover completely with hot water. Close with a lid and set aside. Heat olive oil in a saucepan or wok and stir fry chopped onions for a minute. Now add ginger, garlic, and vegetables of your choice (such as carrots, zucchini, red bell pepper, and broccoli for example). Add some tofu too and fry further for 2-3 minutes. Use 5-spice powder for seasoning. Drain the liquid from the bowl of noodles. After removing all the water, add the noodles into the wok. Add the sauce mixture and mix everything well. Cook for another minute or two and serve hot.

Day 7

*"When diet is wrong, medicine is of no use.
When diet is correct, medicine is of no need."*

- *Ayurvedic proverb*

Creamy Chocolate Shake for Breakfast –

What you need:
- Bananas (2, frozen)
- Strawberries (1/3 cup, frozen)
- Unsweetened cocoa powder (2-3 tbsp.)
- Almond butter (2 tbsp.)
- Flaxseed (1 tbsp.)
- Non-dairy milk (1 ½-2 cups)
- Sweetener
- Ice

What to do:
In a blender, blitz together 2 ripe frozen bananas, 1/3 cup frozen strawberries, 2-3 tbsp. pure unsweetened cocoa powder, 2 tbsp. almond butter (salted), 1 tbsp. flaxseed meal, 1 ½ - 2 cups almond milk or soy milk or coconut milk, a dash of agave nectar or stevia, and some ice cubes. Your shake is ready.

Vegetable and Pesto Sandwich for Lunch –

What you need:
- Zucchini (1 sliced)
- Eggplant (1 sliced)
- Bell pepper (4 oz.)
- Onions (1 chopped)
- Pepper (2 tbsp.)
- Salt (1 tbsp.)
- Olive oil (1 tsp.)
- Pesto (dairy-free, to taste)
- Bread
- Lettuce (1 large leaf)
- Tomato (2 slices)

What to do:
Roast zucchini, eggplant, bell pepper, and onions along with seasoning of pepper, salt and olive oil in an oven until they turn soft and lightly brown. Spread dairy-free pesto on two bread slices and pile on the roasted veggies, tomato slices, and some lettuce leaves. Bring the slices together and your yummy veggie sandwich is ready.

Shepherd's pie for Dinner –

What you need:
- Potatoes (5)
- Salt (2 tsp.)
- Vegan margarine (3 oz.)
- Onions (1 chopped)

- Olive oil (1 tsp.)
- Zucchini (2 sliced)
- Mushrooms (1 cup)
- Carrots (3 chopped)
- Tomato paste (2 cups)
- Canned tomatoes (1 can)
- Stock cube (1)
- Herbs
- Vegan Mince
- Gravy powder (1 package)

What to do:

Boil, peel and mash some potatoes with a little salt and some vegan margarine. Sauté onions with some olive oil in a saucepan until tender and to this add chopped zucchini, mushrooms, and carrots. After the veggies have softened add tomato paste, canned tomatoes, stock cube, herbs and casserole mince and stir well. Make thick gravy with gravy powder and some water and pour into this veggie mix. Cool for about 25-30 minutes. In a baking tray, pour this veggie mixture and layer the mashed potato mix on top. Bake this dish for around 25-30 minutes or until the top is nicely browned.

Day 8

"The future depends on what we do in the present."

-   *Gandhi*

5-ingredient healthy delicious smoothie for breakfast –

What you need:
-   Mixed berries (1 cup, frozen)
-   Spinach (2 handfuls, fresh)
-   Mixed fruit juice (2-3 cups)
-   Banana (1 frozen)
-   Flaxseed (1/4 cup)

What to do:
In a blender, blitz together frozen berry mix, spinach, flaxseed, mixed fruit juice, and a frozen banana and your delicious breakfast smoothie is ready.

Peking Mock "duck" pancakes for lunch –

What you need:
-   Vegan "duck" (12 oz.)
-   Duck sauce (5 tsp.)
-   Vegan pancake batter (1 prepackaged)
-   Onions (1 shredded)

- Cucumber (1 thinly sliced)

What to do:
Thaw the mock duck and put into a baking dish. Slather it with Peking duck sauce and bake for about 30 minutes at 200C. Shred the baked mock duck. Use ready-made vegan pancake batter and cook the pancakes as directed. To serve, take a pancake, layer with Peking duck sauce, add shredded onions, cucumbers, and the mock duck and roll it gently. Your savory pancake is ready to enjoy.

Eggplant and Tomato Pasta for Dinner –

What to use:
- Olive Oil (2 tsp.)
- Onions (1 sliced)
- Garlic (2 cloves, minced)
- Eggplant (1 chopped)
- Balsamic vinegar (2 tsp.)
- Tomatoes (1 canned)
- Tomato Paste (1 can)
- Herbs
- Sun-dried tomatoes (1 cup)
- Chili flakes (1 ½ tsp.)
- Sugar (1 tsp.)
- Water (2 cups)

What to do:
In a large pan, add olive oil and sauté onions and

minced garlic cloves. Add chopped eggplant and balsamic vinegar and cook until the veggies are soft and tender. Now add canned tomatoes, tomato paste, dried herbs, sun-dried tomatoes, chili flakes (if you like, add spice), sugar and some water. Bring this mixture to a full boil and cook it down for about half an hour. Cook the pasta separately and drain the excess water. Add the cooked pasta to the cooked veggie mixture and mix well. Add basil for improved flavor, to taste.

You are halfway done!

Congratulations on making it to the halfway point of the journey. Many try and give up long before even getting to this point, so you are to be congratulated on this. You have shown that you are serious about getting better every day. I am also serious about improving my life, and helping others get better along the way. To do this I need your feedback. Click on the link below and take a moment to let me know how this book has helped you. If you feel there is something missing or something you would like to see differently, I would love to know about it. I want to ensure that as you and I improve, this book continues to improve as well. Thank you for taking the time to ensure that we are all getting the most from each other.

Chapter 4: Meal Plan and Outline Recipes for Block II

Day 9

"Vegan food is soul food in its truest form. Soul food means to feed the soul. And to me, your soul is your intent. If your intent is pure, you are pure."

- *Erykah Bad*

Blueberry maple and protein shake for breakfast –

What to use:
- Low-fat yogurt (3 cups)
- Vanilla protein powder (1 scoop)
- Blueberries (frozen, ½ cup)
- Maple extract (2 tsp.)
- Flaxseed (1/3 cup)
- Ice

What to do:
In a blender, mix low-fat yogurt, 1 scoop of vanilla protein powder, ½ cup blueberries (frozen), maple extract (to taste), flaxseed meal, and some ice cubes. Your delicious and nutritious breakfast shake is ready

Veggie fritters for lunch –

What to use:
- All-purpose flour (2 cups)
- Soy milk (2/3 cup)
- Choice of vegetables (1/2 cup)
- Salt (1 tbsp.)
- Pepper (1 tbsp.)
- Oil (1 tsp.)

What to do:
Mix all-purpose flour and soy milk to form batter for the fritters. Stir in sliced vegetables of your choice (zucchini, carrots, potatoes, broccoli florets, onions) and season with salt and pepper. Heat a little oil in a large skillet and spoon out a little of this mixture at a time giving it a round flat shape. Flip over and cook the other side after one side is cooked. Remove from heat, drain excess oil on tissue paper and serve hot.

Saucy tofu skewers for dinner – Cut out tofu and all your favorite veggies in roughly the same size squares. Place them on a bamboo or metal skewer. Cover with any of your favorite vegan sauces and leave to marinate for some time Barbecue or grill on a skillet until cooked. Serve with extra sauce.

Day 10

"Nothing will benefit human health and increase the chances for survival of life on Earth as much as the evolution to a vegetarian diet."

— Albert Einstein

Kale-based smoothie for breakfast –

What to use:
- Banana (1 whole)
- Mixed berries (frozen, ½ cup)
- Hemp seeds (1 tbsp)
- Kale (2 cups)
- Pomegranate juice (⅔ cup)
- Water

What to do:
In a food blender, blitz together 1 banana (medium ripe), ½ cup mixed berries (frozen), 1 tbsp. hulled hemp seeds, 2 cups kale leaves (fresh or frozen), 2/3 cup pomegranate juice, and some water (depending on the consistency you like; less water if you want a thick smoothie and more water if you want a thin smoothie).

Parsnip and Tempeh Rolls for lunch –

What to use:
- Garlic (1 clove, minced)
- Onions (1 diced)
- Oil (2 tsp.)
- Cumin (1 tbsp.)
- Sage (1 ½ oz.)
- Marjoram (2 oz.)
- Thyme (1 oz.)
- Salt (1 tbsp.)
- Pepper (1 tbsp.)
- Parsnip (2 chopped)
- Tempeh (6 oz.)
- Worcestershire sauce (anchovy-free)
- Water
- Soy sauce (2 tsp.)
- Phyllo pastry sheets

What to do:
Fry garlic and onions in a little oil until soft and add spices including cumin powder, dried sage, marjoram, thyme, salt and pepper and cook until the aromas are released. Add grated parsnip and tempeh to this mixture until soft. Add anchovy-free Worcestershire sauce, water, and soy sauce and cook (stirring continuously) for 4-5 minutes more until the parsnips are fully cooked. Season with salt and pepper and keep aside.

Cut pastry sheets such that you can make rectangle rolls. Spread the tempeh and parsnip filling over the pastry, then fold over the pastry sheet and press the meeting ends together to seal well. Then cut these filled portions into bite-sized pieces. Bake them in a preheated oven at 180C for about 15 minutes or until they are golden brown.

Chili non-carne for dinner -

What to use:
- Onions (1 chopped)
- Garlic (2 cloves, minced)
- Zucchini (1 sliced)
- Carrots (2 sliced)
- Mushrooms (1 cup)
- Bell pepper (1 chopped)
- Cumin (2 tbsp.)
- Coriander (1 tbsp.)
- Fennel seeds (2 tsp.)
- Chili flakes (1 tsp.)
- Peppercorns (1 tbsp.)
- Paprika (1 tbsp.)
- Canned Tomatoes (1 can)
- Tomato Paste (1 can)
- Kidney beans (3 cups)
- Stock cube

What to do:
In a big saucepan, fry onions and garlic until soft. Add zucchini, carrots, mushrooms, and bell pepper and fry some more until veggies are all

tender. Add a spice mixture consisting of cumin powder, coriander powder, fennel seeds, chili flakes, peppercorns, paprika, and salt. Cook for some more time until the spices release aroma. To this add canned tomatoes, tomato paste, kidney beans (canned) and stock cube. Simmer for about half an hour and your non-carne is ready. Serve with rice, baked potatoes, enchiladas, or tacos.

Day 11

"Raw food is the best way to have the cleanest energy. We take so much care about what kind of fuel we put in our car, what kind of oil. We care about that sometimes more than the fuel that we're looking at putting in our bodies. It's cleaner burning fuel."

- *Woody Harrelson*

Mango Green Smoothie for breakfast–

What to use:
- Mango (frozen, 1 ½ cups)
- Strawberries (frozen, 1 cup)
- Spinach (1 cup, fresh)
- Almond milk (1 cup)
- Sweetener

What to do:
In a blender, blitz together 1 ½ cups of frozen mango, 1 cup frozen strawberries, 1 cup spinach (fresh), 1 cup almond milk, and a vegan sweetener like stevia or agave. Your mango green smoothie is ready.

Spicy Couscous for lunch –

What to use:

- Olive oil (2 tsp.)
- Onions (1/2 chopped)
- Garlic (1 clove, minced)
- Bell pepper (1 chopped)
- Zucchini (1 sliced)
- Cumin (1 tsp.)
- Coriander (1 tsp.)
- Pepper (1 tbsp.)
- Fennel (1 tbsp.)
- Chili flakes (1 tbsp.)
- Salt (1 tbsp.)
- Couscous (2 cups)
- Water (boiling)
- Chickpeas (cooked)
- Stock powder (1 package)
- Sun-dried tomatoes (2/3 cup)

What to do:

In a large pan, heat some olive oil and sauté onions and garlic until translucent. Add bell pepper and zucchini and cook until soft. Add spice mixture consisting of cumin, coriander, black pepper, fennel, chili flakes, and salt. Fry for another minute until the aromas of the spices are released. Stir in some couscous and add boiling water and some stock powder into this veggie mixture. Now add some sun-dried tomatoes and cooked chickpeas to this and mix thoroughly. Cover the pan with a lid and put off the heat and let it be for about 5 minutes. Once the couscous has absorbed all the stock, sprinkle some freshly chopped coriander and your lunch is ready.

Thai Red Curry for Dinner –

What to use:
- Onions (1 chopped)
- Red curry paste (2 tsp.)
- Coconut milk (1 cup)
- Vegetable stock (2 cups)
- Tofu (8 oz.)
- Mushrooms (1 cup)
- Sugar (2 tsp.)
- Soy sauce (1 tsp.)
- Bell pepper (1 chopped)
- Bamboo shoots (1/3 cup)
- Chili (2 tsp.)
- Sugar snap peas (2 cups)

What to do:
Fry onions in a little bit of oil until tender. To this add 2 tsp. of red curry paste (ensure that the paste has no shrimp paste in it). Stir for a while and then slowly add coconut milk in small amounts stirring continuously. Now add vegetable stock. Bring this mixture to a boil and then reduce the heat to allow it to simmer.

Add tofu, mushroom, sugar, soy sauce, and bell pepper to this mixture and continue to simmer for 10 more minutes. Now add bamboo shoots, chili, and sugar snap peas and cook for another 5 minutes. Serve with steamed rice.

Day 12

Mango-Strawberry with lime smoothie for breakfast –

What to use:
- Mangoes (2, cubed)
- Strawberries (frozen, ½ cup)
- Lime juice (half lime)
- Ice

What to do:
In a blender, blitz together 2 mangoes (cubed), ½ cup frozen strawberries, lime juice (from half a lime), and ice cubes. Your lime mango-strawberry smoothie is ready.

Asparagus and Pine Nut Tart for lunch –

What to use:
- Pastry sheet
- Mustard (1/2 tsp.)
- Asparagus (5 pieces)
- Vegan cream cheese (1 tsp.)
- Non-dairy milk (1 tbsp)
- Vegan cheese (to taste)

- Pine nuts (1/3 cup)

What to do:
Cut a sheet of pastry into two such as that you have 2 equal rectangles. At ½ cm from the edge, gently score the 4 sides of the pastry. Spread some mustard on the pastry sheet and place 5 asparagus sticks on each of the two rectangles (within the scored line). Bake until the pastry starts to rise. Mix together vegan cream cheese and 1 tbsp. non-dairy milk. Pour this mixture over the pastry and sprinkle some vegan cheese over. Put the pastry in the oven again and bake for about 10 minutes until golden brown. Remove from the oven and sprinkle roasted pine nuts over the tarts. Enjoy.

Tacos and Guacamole for dinner –

What to use:
- Prepared chili non-carne
- Taco size tortillas
- Salad leaf mixture
- Guacamole
- Salsa

What to do:
First, make the chili non-carne (recipe described in Day 10 dinner meal). First, heat the soft taco shells in a skillet and then fill them with salad leaves, guacamole, salsa, and chili non-

carne. Your simple yet delicious taco meal is ready.

Day 13

"Strength does not come from physical capacity. It comes from an indomitable will."
-   Mahatma Gandhi

Jelly Dates and Peanut butter smoothie for breakfast –

What to use:
- Medjool dates (4)
- Peanut butter (1 tbsp.)
- Banana (1 frozen)
- Almond milk (¾ cup)
- Blueberries (frozen, 1/3 cup)
- Flaxseed (1 tbsp.)

What to do:
In a blender, blitz together 4 Medjool dates, 1 tbsp. peanut butter, 1 frozen banana, ¾ cup almond milk, 1/3 cup frozen blueberries, and 1 tbsp. flaxseed meal. Blend until desired smooth consistency. Your jelly dates and peanut butter smoothie is ready for enjoyment.

Pumpkin soup for lunch –

What to use:
- Oil
- Onions (1 chopped)

- Pumpkin squash (2 chunked)
- Water (boiling)
- Noodle soup packet (1 package)
- Salt (1 tsp.)
- Pepper (1 tsp.)

What to do:

In a large pan, heat up some oil and sauté onions and pumpkin squash chunks until they start to brown. Pour boiling water until the veggies are completely covered and then stir in 1 packet of noodle soup. Simmer the pan contents until the pumpkin squash is cooked through. Blend this entire mixture and season with salt and pepper. Serve with some crusty bread.

Marinated Tempeh Steak with Veggies for dinner –

What to use:
- Tempeh (4 blocks)
- Garlic (1 clove, minced)
- Soy sauce (2 tsp.)
- Oil (2 tsp.)
- Pine nuts (1/3 cup)
- Asparagus (6 oz.)
- Baby potatoes (2 cups)
- Vegan margarine
- Parsley (1/3 cup)

What to do:

Slice the tempeh block into two thinner pieces and then cut these again so that you get 4 blocks of tempeh altogether. Marinate these tempeh blocks with garlic-infused soy sauce for as long as you can. Drizzle some oil in a skillet and fry the marinated tempeh until both the sides are brown.

For the veggies, roast pine nuts and steam the asparagus spears. Steam baby potatoes until they are soft. Toss the boiled potatoes with some vegan margarine in a hot skillet and chopped parsley. Plate the tempeh and arrange all the veggies on the side.

Day 14

"Energy and persistence conquer all things."

- *Benjamin Franklin*

Berry, Banana, and Sesame Smoothie for breakfast –

What to use:
- Banana (1 whole)
- Wheat germ (4 tbsp.)
- Sesame seeds (4 tbsp)
- Strawberries (fresh, 5)
- Yogurt (berry flavored, 2 tbsp)

What to do:
Put 1 small banana, 1 tbsp. wheat germ, 4 tbsp. of sesame seeds, 5 strawberries, and 2 tbsp. of berry-flavored yogurt and blend until smooth. Pour into a glass and have a wholesome vegan breakfast.

Tempeh strips with salad wraps for lunch –

What to use:
- Tempeh (12 oz.)
- Garlic (2 cloves, minced)
- Canola oil (1 tbsp.)

- Sesame oil (1 tsp.)
- Vegan margarine (1 tsp.)
- Beetroot dip (3 tsp.)
- Wrap
- Fresh veggies of choice

What to do:
Marinate tempeh with a garlic infused mixture of canola and sesame oils. After marination, cut into strips and cook in a hot skillet until both sides are brown. Spread vegan margarine and beetroot dip on the ready-to-eat wraps and fill the wraps with tempeh strips and your veggies (cut into strips).

Lentil Dahl for dinner –

What to use:
- Garlic (1 clove, minced)
- Onion (1 chopped)
- Vegetable oil (2 tsp.)
- Cumin (1 tbsp.)
- Ginger (2 tbsp. grated)
- Turmeric (1 tbsp.)
- Garam masala (1 tbsp.)
- Lentils (2 cups)
- Cardamom pods
- Stock powder
- Cinnamon (1 tbsp.)
- Bay leaves

What to do:
In a saucepan, fry garlic and onions in a little bit of vegetable oil until onions are translucent. Add cumin, ginger, turmeric powder, and garam masala powder and continue to fry until the aromas of the spices are released. Now add some water, lentils, cardamom pods, stock powder, cinnamon powder, and bay leaves. Cook, while stirring occasionally, for about 25 minutes until the mixture is fully cooked. Serve hot with rice or your favorite crusty bread.

You are halfway done!

Congratulations on making it to the halfway point of the journey. Many try and give up long before even getting to this point, so you are to be congratulated on this. You have shown that you are serious about getting better every day. I am also serious about improving my life and helping others get better along the way. To do this I need your feedback. Click on the link below and take a moment to let me know how this book has helped you. If you feel there is something missing or something you would like to see differently, I would love to know about it. I want to ensure that, as you and I improve, this book continues to improve as well. Thank you for taking the time to ensure that we are all getting the most from each other.

http://viewbook.at/veganbook

Day 15

Cheesecake strawberry smoothie for breakfast –

What to use:
- Strawberries (1 cup)
- Oil
- Vegan Cottage cheese (1 cup)
- Chia seeds (1/3 cup)
- Sweetener
- Ice

What to do:
First, roast the strawberries with any vegetable oil and bake for about 20 minutes until the juices of the berries are released. Now, in a blender, blitz together cottage cheese, roasted strawberries, chia seeds, a sweetener like an agave or stevia, and ice cubes. Pour the smoothie into a glass and enjoy your breakfast.

Vegetable burger and raw salad for lunch –

What to use:

- Prepared vegetable or bean burger patty
- Fresh vegetables and leafy greens
- Lime juice (to taste)
- Agave (to taste)

What to do:
Heat up a ready-to-eat vegetable or red lentil burger until brown on both sides. Chop up some favorite vegetables like cucumber, tomatoes, cabbage, and baby spinach and make a salad with a simple lime juice and agave dressing. Enjoy your lunch of vegetable burger and salad.

Roast with cooked Vegetables for dinner
–

What to use:
- Potatoes (2 diced)
- Butternut squash (1 diced)
- Zucchini (2 chopped)
- Carrots (3 chopped)
- Corn
- Onions (1 chopped)
- Garlic (2 cloves minced)
- Rosemary
- Bell pepper (3 chopped)
- Vegan roast

What to do:

In a greased baking pan, place potatoes, butternut squash, zucchini, carrots, corn, onions, and garlic and sprinkle some rosemary over. Cover the pan with aluminum foil and bake at 180C in a preheated oven for about 30 minutes. Remove the vegan roast from the packet and rub with olive oil, rosemary, and mint. Once the veggies have cooked for 30 minutes, place the roast in the middle, add some bell pepper and bake for another half hour. Serve with garlic bread and a mushroom gravy.

Day 16

"Motivation is what gets you started. Habit is what keeps you going."

- *Jim Ryan*

Raspberry-banana smoothie for breakfast –

What to use:
- *Banana (1 frozen)*
- Raspberries (frozen, 1 ¼ cup)
- Orange juice (¾ cup)
- Pomegranate juice (½ cup)
- Almond milk (unsweetened, ¾ cup)

What to do:
In a food processor, blend together 1 large, ripe banana (frozen), 1 ¼ cup raspberry (frozen), ¾ cup orange juice, ½ cup pomegranate juice, and ¾ cup unsweetened almond milk. Your raspberry-banana smoothie is ready.

Sweet corn and cauliflower soup for lunch –

What to use:
- Cauliflower head (1/2)
- Corn on cob (2)

- Potato (1 large, diced)
- Leek (1)
- Vegetable stock (1 cup)
- Salt (1 tbsp.)
- Pepper (1 tbsp.(
- Water (2 cups)

What to do:
In a big saucepan, put a ½ head of cauliflower (cut into florets), kernels from 2 corn cobs, 1 large potato (diced), 1 small leek, 1 cup of vegetable stock, salt, and pepper and one liter of water. Bring this mixture to a boil and then simmer on a low flame for about 15-20 minutes until veggies are cooked through. Cool and then blend in a food processor. Serve hot with crusty bread.

Spaghetti Bolognese for dinner –

What to use:
- Onions (1/2 chopped)
- Garlic (1 clove minced)
- Mushrooms (1 cup)
- Zucchini (1 sliced)
- Carrots (2 chopped)
- Tomatoes (canned)
- Worcestershire sauce (2 tsp. anchovy free)
- Tomato paste (1 can)
- Stock cube

- Herbs
- Spaghetti (1 box)

What to do:

In a large saucepan, fry onions and garlic with some oil until soft. Now add mushrooms, zucchini, and carrots, stir gently and cook for 2-3 minutes. Now add canned tomatoes, anchovy-free Worcestershire sauce, tomato paste, stock cube, and herbs and mix well. Season the mixture with salt and pepper. Simmer for about 20 minutes. Cook and drain spaghetti as directed on the packet and serve with the sauce.

Chapter 5: Meal Plan and Recipes for Block III

"Clear your mind of can't."

- *Samuel Johnson*

Day 17

Peach Oat Smoothie for breakfast –

What to use:
- Peaches (2 cubed)
- Chia seeds (1 tbsp)
- Banana (1/2)
- Uncooked oats (¼ cup)
- Almond milk (unsweetened, ½ cup)
- Orange juice ¼ cup
- Agave (optional)

What to do:
In a blender, blitz together 2 ripe peaches (cut into cubes), 1 tbsp. chia seeds, ½ frozen banana, ¼ cup uncooked oats, ½ cup almond milk (unsweetened), ¼ orange juice, and agave (if you want). Your peach oat smoothie is done.

Stir Fry Veggies and Tempeh with rice for lunch –

What to use:
- Oil (1 tsp.)
- Stir fry vegetables (2 cups)
- Choice of spices
- Tempeh (1 ½ cups)
- Soy sauce (2 tsp.)
- Sweet chili sauce (1 tsp.)

What to do:
Place some oil in a large pan and stir fry vegetables of your choice such as broccoli florets, carrots, zucchini, mushrooms, onions, and whatever else you like to stir fry. Add spices like curry powder, cumin powder, and coriander powder and continue to stir fry until all veggies are tender. Add some tempeh (cut into squares) and then add a mixture of soy sauce and sweet chili sauce. Toss everything together and serve on a plate of steamed hot rice.

Soy strips Rougaille with a watercress salad for dinner –

What to use:
- Olive Oil (2 tsp.)
- Onions (1 chopped)
- Garlic (1 clove minced)
- Thyme
- Ginger (1 oz.)
- Tomato paste (1 can)

- Tomatoes (1 diced)
- Chili (1 tsp.)
- Soy strips (1 package)
- Watercress (3 oz.)
- Carrots (2 chopped)
- Bell pepper (2 chopped)
- Orange juice (1/3 cup)
- Salt (1 tbsp.)
- Pepper (1 tbsp.

What to do:
In a large pan, heat some oil and sauté onions, garlic, thyme, and some ginger. Add tomato paste, tomatoes, and some chili and let it simmer for 2 minutes. In another pan, fry marinated soy strips in olive oil until brown. To the simmering sauce add the fried soy strips with some water and bring to a boil. Then reduce the heat and allow it to simmer for about 10 minutes or until the sauce thickens. For the watercress salad, toss together chopped watercress, carrots, and bell pepper along with vinaigrette of orange juice, salt, and pepper. Place the salad on a plate, and over this, place the sauce-filled soy strips. Enjoy your dinner!

Day 18

Banana bread smoothie for breakfast –

What to use:
- Banana (1 frozen)
- Quinoa (cooked, ½ cup)
- Walnuts (1 tbsp.)
- Flaxseed (2 tbsp.)
- Date (1)
- Cinnamon (¾ tsp.)
- Ice

What to do:
Place 1 frozen banana, ½ cup quinoa (cooked), 1 tbsp. walnuts. 2 tbsp. flaxseed, 1 Medjool date, ¾ tsp cinnamon powder, and some ice cubes. Blitz together, pour into your glass and enjoy your smoothie.

Crispy Mock Chicken with Potato Mash for lunch –

What to use:

- Mock chicken breast (1 prepackaged)
- Oil
- Mashed Potatoes (4 potatoes, mashed)

What to do:
Cut "mock" chicken into chunks or strips and put them into a Ziploc pouch along with seasoning and breadcrumbs for about 30 minutes. Heat some oil in a pan, and fry this in batches until golden brown. Serve on a plate of hot mashed potatoes.

Avocado on Toast for dinner –

What to use:
- Bread
- Vegan margarine
- Avocados (2 whole)
- Fresh veggies (optional)

What to do:
Take a slice of your favorite bread and toast with some vegan margarine until golden brown. Pile mashed avocados over this and enjoy a healthy and extremely easy-to-make vegan meal. You could add some sprouts and raw veggies for some crunch and extra energy.

Day 19

"Setting goals is the first step in turning the invisible into the visible."

- *Tony Robbins*

Green Apple and Cucumber Smoothie for breakfast –

What to use:
- Green apple (1 chopped)
- Walnuts (1 tbsp.)
- Cucumber (1/2)
- Avocado (1/4)
- Agave (optional)
- Ice

What to do:
In a blender, blitz together chopped green apple, 1 tbsp. walnuts, ½ a cucumber, ¼ of an avocado (chopped), some agave (if you want), and ice cubes. Your delicious green apple and cucumber smoothie is ready.

Enchiladas and Guacamole for lunch –

What to use:
- Prepared chili non-carne
- Tortillas (1 package)

- Salsa (4 oz.)
- Guacamole (6 oz.)

What to do:
First, make some chili non-carne as described in an earlier meal plan day (specifically Day 10's dinner recipe). Get yourself some ready-made tortillas and salsa, or create your own salsa by running onions, tomatoes, garlic, jalapenos or chili of choice, lime juice and fresh cilantro through a food processor. On a tortilla, spread some chili non-carne, and fold it over. Bake until the tortillas are slightly brown. Remove from the oven and place some salsa on top. Serve hot with some fresh guacamole.

Bombay potatoes with pita bread for dinner –

What to use:
- Bombay potato packet (1 prepackaged)
- Pita bread
- Vegan sour cream (3 oz.)
- Coriander (1 oz.)

What to do:
Heat the packet of Bombay potatoes and cook as directed. Warm the pita bread and spread the potatoes in a layer on the top. Garnish the pita with some vegan sour cream and some fresh coriander. Dig right in.

Day 20

Strawberries smoothie for breakfast –

What to use:
- Strawberries (frozen, 1 cup)
- Chia seeds (1/3 cup)
- Flaxseed (1/3 cup)
- Oats (2/3 cup)
- Apple cider vinegar (2 tsp.)
- Vanilla extract (2 tbsp.)
- Ice

What to do:
Place 1 cup frozen strawberries, some chia seeds, some flaxseed, raw oats, apple cider vinegar, vanilla extract, and some ice cubes. Blitz all together with a blender and your smoothie is ready.

Roasted vegetable lasagna for lunch –

What to use:
- Eggplant (1 chopped)
- Bell pepper (2 chopped)

- Zucchini (1 chopped)
- Onions (1 chopped)
- Olive oil (2 tsp.)
- Salt (1 tbsp.)
- Pepper (1 tbsp.)
- Pesto
- Tomatoes(2 diced)
- Tomato paste (1 can)
- Vegan margarine
- Flour (2/3 cup)
- Vegan cream cheese (1/3 cup)
- Lasagna noodles (1 package)

What to do:

In a baking dish, put together chopped eggplant, bell pepper, zucchini, and onions. Drizzle some olive oil and season vegetable mixture with salt and pepper. Toss it all together and bake in a medium heated oven until tender. Once this is cooled, add pesto, chopped tomatoes, and tomato paste and mix thoroughly.

Make a white sauce with vegan margarine, flour, and vegan cream cheese. Now, take a baking dish, make a vegetable layer at the bottom; next place a lasagna sheet, and then pour the white sauce over. Repeat this layering process until the ingredients are all used up. Bake for about 30-40 minutes until the top is lightly brown. Enjoy your vegan lasagna hot.

One-pot Black Bean Chili for dinner-

What to use:
- Carrots (2 chopped)
- Peppers (2 chopped)
- Onion (1 chopped)
- Diced tomatoes (1 diced)
- Cumin (1 tsp.)
- Garlic (1 clove, minced)
- Paprika (1 tsp.)
- Chili powder (1 tsp.)
- Black beans (1 ½ cups)
- Corn (1 cup, frozen)
- Vegan cheese (optional)

What to do:
In a large pan sauté carrots, peppers, and onion until tender. After sautéed add diced tomatoes and seasonings such as cumin, garlic, paprika and chili powder. Mix these ingredients well and add in black beans and corn kernels. Let simmer a while before eating for spices to fully blend flavors. Distribute to a bowl and top with vegan cheese, served most deliciously with crusty bread or a baked potato.

Day 21

"Outstanding people have one thing in common: An absolute sense of mission."

- *Zig Ziglar*

Green Smoothie for breakfast –

What to use:
- Cucumber (1)
- Spinach (3 cups, raw)
- Melon (2 cups)
- Green tea (1 cup)
- Lemon juice (1 tsp.)
- Agave (optional)
- Ice

What to do:
Blend together 1 cucumber (diced), 3 cups of spinach (raw), 2 cups melon (cubed), some brewed green tea, a little lemon juice (for tartness), some agave (if you want), and some ice cubes. Once nicely blended pour into a glass and enjoy your breakfast.

Stir-fry vegetables with marinated soy strips for lunch –

What to use:

- Oil
- Favorite vegetables
- Soy strips (marinated)
- Seasonings and sauce of choice

What to do:
In a large pan, with a little oil, stir-fry all your favorite veggies along with some marinated soy strips. Add spices and sauces of your choice. Serve on a plate of hot steamed rice.

Vegan hot dogs for dinner –

What to use:
- Vegan hot dogs (2)
- Vegan margarine
- Bun (2)
- Mustard (to taste)
- Cucumber (1/2 thinly sliced)
- Tomato (1/2 thinly sliced)
- Lettuce (a few leaves)

What to do:
Cook the ready-made vegan hot dogs by boiling, steaming, or frying. Spread vegan margarine on one side of the bun (cut in half), smear mustard on the other half, place the hot dogs in the middle and pile on cucumbers and tomato slices and some lettuce leaves. Bring the two halves of the bun together and your dinner is ready.

Day 22

"Nothing is impossible; the word itself says 'I'm possible!'"

- *Audrey Hepburn*

Mint and chocolate chip smoothie for breakfast –

What to use:
- Peppermint tea (1 cup)
- Almond milk (1 cup, unsweetened)
- Banana (1 frozen)
- Spinach (2 cups, fresh)
- Hemp seeds (1 tsp)
- Chocolate chips (1/3 cup)
- Ice

What to do:
Place a peppermint tea in boiling water and get a nicely concentrated cup of peppermint tea ready. In a blender, put together 1 cup unsweetened almond milk, 1 frozen banana, 2 cups of spinach, 1 tsp. of hemp seeds, 1/3 cup of chocolate chips, and ice cubes. Blitz everything and pour into a glass. Put some more chocolate chips on top and your breakfast is ready.

Thai noodles for lunch –

What to use:
- Vermicelli noodles (1 package)
- Olive oil
- Chopped stir fry vegetables of choice (2 cups)
- Soy sauce (1 tsp.)
- Sesame oil (1 tsp.)

What to do:
Cook vermicelli noodles as directed on the packet. Drain and keep aside. Heat some olive oil in a large pan and add chopped veggies like celery, bok choy, spring onions, mushrooms, peanuts, chili, ginger, and garlic. Cook until the vegetables are tender. Make a mixture of light soy sauce and sesame oil. Once the vegetables are nicely tender, stir in the noodles and add the sauce mixture. Mix well. Remove from heat and serve hot.

Sandwich with soy strips for dinner –

What to use:
- Bread
- Marinated soy strips (1 package)
- Raw vegetables of choice (sliced)
- Vegan margarine
- Dijon mustard (to taste)

What to do:

Make a yummy sandwich with your favorite bread slices and marinated soy strips. Add some raw vegetables for some crunch. You can use vegan margarine and Dijon mustard as sandwich spreads and dig right in.

Day 23

"The successful warrior is the average man, with laser-like focus."

- *Bruce Lee*

Apple Smoothie for breakfast –

What to use:
- Apple (1)
- Cherries (½ cup, pitted)
- Cucumber (1/2)
- Raspberries (½ cup)
- Chia seeds (1 tsp.)
- Ice

What to do:
Blitz together 1 apple, ½ cup cherries, ½ cucumber, ½ cup raspberries, 1 tsp chia seeds, and some ice cubes. Pour into your favorite glass and enjoy the apple smoothie.

Borscht for lunch –

What to use:
- Beetroots (4)
- Oil
- Celery (3 stalks, chopped)
- Carrots (2 chopped)

- Mushrooms (1 cup)
- Leeks (3)
- Water

What to do:
Cook and peel beetroots. Grate half of it and thinly slice the remaining. In a large pan, heat oil, and add chopped celery, carrots, mushrooms, leeks and some water. Bring to a boil; add the grated beets, reduce the heat and simmer for about 10 minutes. In another pan, take some more water and boil the sliced beets and simmer on a medium heat for not more than 10 minutes. Drain out the beetroot slices (which you can discard) and pour the beetroot-infused juice into the other simmering veggie mixture. Remove from heat. Season with spices of your choice and your yummy borscht is ready.

Vegan prawns and some salad for dinner –
What to use:
- Mock prawns (prepackaged)
- Soy sauce (1 tsp.)
- Raw vegetables of choice (3 cups)
- Dressing or sauce of choice (to taste)

What to do:
In a hot skillet, fry the mock prawns with some oil. Sprinkle soy sauce over the mock prawn. Serve hot with crunchy veggies, tossed with a

dressing of your choice.

Chapter 6: Meal Plan and Recipes for Block IV

Day 24

"Be miserable. Or motivate yourself. Whatever has to be done, it's always your choice."

-   Wayne Dyer

Blueberries smoothie for breakfast –

What to use:
- Non-dairy milk (1 ½ cups)
- Oats (2 tbsp.)
- Vanilla Protein powder (1 tsp.)
- Vanilla extract
- Chia seeds (1 tsp.)
- Blueberries (fresh, ½ cup)

What to do:
This needs a little bit of planning the night before. Combine 1 ½ cups of any non-dairy milk, 2 tbsp. of oats, 1 tsp. of vanilla protein powder, a little vanilla extract and 1 tsp. of chia seeds. Place in the fridge the night before. In the morning, blitz this mixture along with ½ cup blueberries and your smoothie is ready.

Tempeh Cottage Pie for lunch –

What to use:
- Cumin seeds (1 tsp.)
- Onion (1 chopped)
- Garlic (2 cloves minced)
- Capers (2/3 cup)
- Tempeh (1 ½ cups)
- Carrots (2 chopped)
- Tomatoes (1 diced)
- Corn (1 cob)
- Peas (5 oz.)
- Sweet Potato (1)
- Water
- Tomato paste (1 can)
- Salt (1 tsp.)
- Pepper (2 tbsp.)
- Potatoes (2)
- Soy milk (1/3 cup)
- Vegan margarine

What to do:
Fry cumin seeds, onions, garlic, and capers until tender. Put in the tempeh and fry for a couple of minutes more. Add carrots, tomatoes, corn, peas, and sweet potato and cook for another 2-3 minutes. Add water and tomato paste; bring to a boil, reduce heat and simmer until the liquid reduces, but ensure that the mixture does not get too dry. Add salt and pepper for seasoning.

Nicely mash par-boiled potatoes with soymilk and vegan margarine. Season this with salt and pepper. Pour the tempeh mixture onto a baking tray and evenly spread it out. Spread the mashed potato mixture over this layer and sprinkle paprika over the potatoes. Bake in a medium heated oven for 45 minutes until the potato layer is golden brown.

San Choy Bow for dinner –

What to use:
- Onion (1/2 chopped)
- Garlic (1 clove minced)
- Ginger (1 root grated)
- Chili (1 tsp.)
- Mushrooms (1 cup)
- Vegan mince (1 package)
- Vegetable stock (1 cup)
- Coriander (1 tsp.)
- Soy sauce (2 tsp.)
- Lime juice (2 tbsp.)

What to do:
In a large wok, stir-fry onion, and garlic over a high heat. Add ginger, chili, and mushrooms and continue stir-frying for another 3 minutes. Mix in the vegan mince and stir-fry for some a few more minutes breaking down the lumps in the mince as you go along. Add stock and bring to a boil. Reduce heat and continue to simmer

until the stock is fully absorbed. Stir in coriander, soy sauce, and some lime juice. Serve hot on a platter of lettuce leaves.

Day 25

"I believe that the greatest gift you can give to the world and your family is a healthy you."

- *Joyce Meyer*

Raspberry lemon smoothie for breakfast –

What to use:
- Non-dairy milk (1 ½ cups)
- Raspberries (½ cup)
- Oats (2 tbsp.)
- Lemon juice (1 tbsp.)
- Chia seeds (1 tbsp.)
- Almond butter (1 tbsp.)
- Lemon zest
- Vanilla extract
- Stevia leaf powder

What to do:
This requires you to prepare the ingredients the night before. Combine 1 ½ cups of non-dairy milk, 1/2 cup of raspberry, 2 tbsp. oats, 1 tbsp. lemon juice, 1 tbsp. of chia seeds, 1 tbsp. of almond butter, a little lemon zest, vanilla extract, and stevia powder. Place in the fridge overnight. In the morning, blitz this mixture in a blender until smooth. Your smoothie is ready.

Vegetable curry with rice for lunch –

What to use:
- *Vegetable oil*
- Onions (1 chopped)
- Cumin seeds (2 tsp.)
- Garlic (1 clove minced)
- Potatoes (2)
- Cauliflower (1 head)
- Carrots (3 chopped)
- Mushrooms (1 ½ cups)
- French beans (2 cups)
- Peas (2 cups)
- Curry paste
- Turmeric (1 tsp.)
- Coriander (1 tsp.)
- Salt (2 tbsp.)
- Pepper (1 tbsp.)

What to do:
In a pan, heat some vegetable oil, and fry onions, garlic, and cumin seeds until onions are translucent. Add chopped vegetables including potatoes, cauliflower, carrots, mushrooms, French beans, and peas. Add curry paste, turmeric powder, and coriander powder. Sprinkle a little water and cook until the veggies are tender all the way through. Season the curry with salt and pepper. Serve hot on a layer of steamed rice.

Potato and vegetable salad for dinner –

What to use:
- Potatoes (3 steamed)
- Dijon mustard (1/3 cup)
- Vegan mayo (2/3 cup)
- Carrots (3 grated)
- Onions (1 chopped)

What to do:
Steam potatoes and keep aside. Make a sauce by mixing Dijon mustard and vegan mayonnaise. Cut the potatoes and stir in some grated carrots and finely chopped onions. Stir in the sauce. Mix thoroughly and your salad is ready to be polished off.

Day 26

"To keep the body in good health is a duty...otherwise we shall not be able to keep our mind strong and clear."

- *Buddha*

Blueberry peach smoothie for breakfast –

What to use:
- Peach (1/2)
- Blueberries (1 cup)
- Protein powder (1 scoop)
- Green tea (1 cup)
- Chia seeds (1 tsp.)
- Probiotics
- Ice

What to do:
Blend together 1/2 a peach, 1 cup blueberries, 1 scoop protein powder, 1 cup prepared green tea, 1 tsp. chia seeds, 1 serving probiotics, and some ice cubes in a blender until smooth. Enjoy your breakfast.

Stuffed tofu turkey for lunch –

What to use:

- Firm tofu (prepackaged)
- Tamari oil (1 tsp.)
- Olive oil (1 tsp.)
- Garlic (1 clove crushed)
- Onions (1 chopped)
- Mushrooms (2 cups)
- Celery (4 stalks)
- Sesame oil (2 tsp.)
- Rosemary
- Thyme
- Sage
- Pepper (2 tbsp.)
- Soy sauce (2 tsp.)
- Breadcrumbs (prepackaged)

What to do:
You will need a large amount of firm tofu (about 2 kg). Crumble the firm tofu and add a marinade consisting of tamari oil, olive oil, and 2 cloves of crushed garlic. Stir well and keep aside. Tightly pack this tofu in a cheesecloth-lined colander and place cheesecloth over this too. Place a heavy object on top of this arrangement and let it rest for about an hour.

For the stuffing, fry onions, garlic, mushrooms, and celery in sesame oil. Add rosemary, thyme, dried sage, black pepper, and some soy sauce and cook until the vegetables are soft. Remove from heat. Add some breadcrumbs and mix well.

Remove the heavy object and the cheesecloth from the top of the tofu arrangement. Using a big ladle, scoop out tofu from the top such that about an inch of tofu is left on three sides. Press the stuffing into this hollow and put back the scooped tofu on top and press down firmly on all sides. Turn this over onto a greased baking dish and remove the other cheesecloth too. Bake the stuffed tofu for an hour until the top is nice and brown. Remove from the oven and cool. Your stuffed tofu is ready to be carved.

Zucchini fritters for dinner –

What to use:
- Zucchini (3)
- All-Purpose Flour (2/3 cup)
- Salt (1 tsp.)
- Pepper (2 tbsp.)
- Breadcrumbs (1/3 cup)
- Herbs
- Oil

What to do:
Cut zucchini into baton shapes. Make a batter with all-purpose flour and season this with salt and pepper. Make a mixture of breadcrumbs and herbs. Dip the zucchini into the batter, then coat with the breadcrumb mixture and deep fry in hot oil. Serve hot with any sauce or chutney.

Day 27

"There's nothing more important than our good health- that's our principal capital asset."

- *Arlen Specter*

Pumpkin banana smoothie for breakfast
–

What to use:
- Almond milk (1 cup)
- Banana (1/2)
- Pumpkin (canned, ½ cup)
- Maple syrup (½ tsp)
- Vanilla Extract
- Ginger (ground)
- All Spice
- Ice

What to do:
Blend together 1 cup almond milk, ½ banana, ½ cup canned pumpkin, ½ tsp maple syrup, vanilla extract, a little ground ginger, a pinch of all spice powder, and ice cubes in a food processor. When a thick, smooth consistency is reached, you can gulp down your smoothie.

Spanakopita for lunch –

What to use:
- Onions (1 chopped)
- Garlic (1 clove minced)
- Spinach (2 cups, cooked, chopped)
- Mushroom (1 cup)
- Tofu (5 oz.)
- Pine nuts (1/3 cup, roasted)
- Salt (1 tbsp.)
- Pepper (1 tbsp.)
- Vegan margarine
- Phyllo dough (prepackaged)

What to do:
Make a filling with sautéed onions, garlic, cooked and chopped spinach, mushrooms, tofu, and some roasted pine nuts. Season the filling with salt and pepper. Use this filling to make rolls using ready-made phyllo pastry dough. Place the rolls on a greased baking dish and brush them with melted margarine. Bake for about 15 minutes at 350 degrees or until golden brown. Serve warm with a vegan dip.

Vegan sushi for dinner –

What to use:
- Sushi rice (2 cups)
- Sugar (1 tbsp.)
- Rice vinegar (3 tsp.)
- Nori (seaweed sheet)
- Filling choice (optional)

What to do:

Cook rinsed sushi rice until the water is all absorbed. Stir in sugar and rice vinegar with the cooked rice and mix such that there are no lumps. Keep this aside. On a nori sheet, spread this rice evenly with enough space for any filling too. Other fillings to be considered may be avocado, carrots or cucumbers, julienned and placed to roll with the rice. Ensure you do not fill the nori wrapper too much, as then you would not be able to roll the sheets cleanly. Using a rolling mat, roll the sushi-filled nori sheet and then remove the mat and cut into bite-sized pieces.

Day 28

"The foundation of success in life is good health: that is the substratum fortune; it is also the basis of happiness. A person cannot accumulate a fortune very well when he is sick."

- P. T. Barnum

Caramel apple green smoothie for breakfast –

What to use:
- Apple (1 diced, frozen)
- Almond milk (2 cups)
- Spinach (2 cups)
- Peanut butter (2 tbsp.)
- Dates (2)
- Cinnamon
- Ice

What to do:
In a blender, put 1 frozen apple (diced), 2 cups almond milk, 2 cups spinach, 2 tbsp. peanut butter, 2 dates, ground cinnamon, and ice cubes and blitz together. Your smoothie is ready.

Asparagus and Mushroom Risotto for lunch –

What to use:
- Stock powder (prepackaged)
- Water
- Onion powder (1 tsp.)
- Mushrooms (1 cup)
- Dried herbs
- Vegan margarine
- Onions (1/2 chopped)
- Olive oil
- Rice (2/3 cup)
- Wine
- Vegetable stock (1 cup)

What to do:
In a large pan, mix water, stock powder, onion powder, mushrooms, and choice of dried herbs. Bring the pan to a boil and then reduce to a simmer. In another pan, melt vegan margarine with a little olive oil on a medium heat. Cook the onions until they are translucent and then add rice and stir continuously. To this rice, add wine and stir again. When the wine is completely gone, spoon in a ladle of vegetable stock. Now add the mushroom mixture. Keep adding stock as it continuously gets absorbed. Repeat this until you get the desired risotto consistency. Serve hot.

Mexican Beans and Baked Potato for dinner –

What to use:
- Potatoes (3)
- Mexican beans (3 cups)

What to do:
Poke potatoes through with a fork and then place in a microwave for about 5 minutes, depending on size, so that it is not cooked through. Then cook in an oven until it is crisp on the outside and soft on the inside. Using pre-bought Mexican beans, heat up in a saucepan. If you would like to make homemade Mexican beans and have time for some extra prep, take pre-soaked pinto beans and season with sautéed garlic, onion and olive oil over medium heat. Add green chili, diced tomatoes, vegetable broth and then water until beans are covered. Bring to low boil, then allow to sit in simmer until beans are tender. Season with a choice of seasonings to personal taste and stir, cooking for a few more minutes until flavors are absorbed. Place the beans over the cooked potatoes and enjoy your meal.

Day 29

"Food is really and truly the most effective medicine."

— Joel Fuhrman

Ultra Green smoothie for breakfast –

What to use:
- Spinach (2 cups)
- Coconut milk (unsweetened, 1 cup)
- Banana (1/2 frozen)
- Avocado (1/2 frozen)
- Hemp seeds (2 tsp.)
- Ice

What to do:
In a food processor, place 2 cups spinach, 1 cup unsweetened coconut milk, ½ a frozen banana, ½ a frozen avocado, 2 tsp. of hemp seeds, and ice cubes. Blitz all the ingredients together until you get a thick smoothie. Enjoy it.

Vegan pizza for lunch –

What to use:
- Vegan pizza crust (prepackaged)
- Vegan cheese (2 cups)

- Red bell pepper (strips)
- Green bell pepper (strips)
- Mushrooms (sliced)
- Olives

What to do:
Buy a ready-made vegan pizza crust base and layer it with vegan cheese, thin strips of red bell pepper, green bell pepper, sliced mushrooms, and olives over a layer of vegan pizza sauce, measured to taste. Bake for about 10-15 minutes.

Lentils, Leek, and Potato Soup for dinner
–

What to use:
- Potatoes (2 chopped)
- Leeks (4)
- Red lentils (½ cup)
- Water
- Stock powder (prepackaged)
- Salt (1 tsp.)
- Pepper (2 tbsp.)

What to do:
Take chopped potatoes, leeks, and ½ cup of red lentils along with water and stock powder in a large pan. Bring it to a boil and then simmer on medium heat. Once cooked and cooled, blend in a food processor. Add a little hot water if you

want a thinner consistency. Season the soup with salt and pepper.

Day 30

"The finish line is just the beginning of a whole new race."

- *Unknown*

Chocolate and Raspberry smoothie for breakfast –

What to use:
- Almond milk (1 cup)
- Spinach (2 cups)
- Raspberries (1 cup)
- Coconut (shredded, 2 tbsp.)
- Cocoa powder (unsweetened, 1 tbsp.)
- Ice

What to do:
Blend together 1 cup almond milk, 2 cups spinach, 1 cup raspberries, 2 tbsp. shredded coconut, 1 tbsp. cocoa powder, and some ice cubes in a food processor until you get a smooth consistency. Enjoy your smoothie.

Fried rice for lunch –

What to use:
- Onions (1/2 chopped)
- Fresh, chopped vegetables (2/3 cup)

- Soy sauce (2 tsp.)
- Sweet chili sauce (1 tsp.)
- Rice (2/3 cup)
- Salt (1 tsp.)
- Pepper (2 tbsp.)

What to do:
Heat oil in a large pan and sauté chopped onions. Add finely chopped veggies of your choice, with the recipe generally including cauliflower, French beans, peas, cabbage, and corn kernels. Add a sauce mixture of soy sauce and sweet chili sauce to this, measuring to taste, and cook until the veggies are tender. Add the desired amount of cooked rice and toss and mix thoroughly. Season the fried rice with salt and pepper if needed. Serve hot.

Antipasto Pasta Salad for dinner –

What to use:
- Pasta (1 box)
- Bell pepper (1)
- Onions (1/2 chopped)
- Carrots (2 chopped)
- Cucumber (1 sliced)
- Kalamata olives (1/3 cup)
- Balsamic vinegar (2 tsp.)
- Additional fresh vegetables

What to do:

Cook choice of pasta as per directions on the packet. Mix together thinly diced bell pepper, onions, carrots, cucumber, and kalamata olives with some balsamic vinegar and choice of vegetables such as zucchini and tomato to create your antipasto salsa. Add the cooked pasta and toss all the ingredients together until pasta is well covered. Your salad is ready.

Conclusion – How to Stay Committed

If you are trying to change your lifestyle, it calls for immense commitment and hard work. It is quite easy to fall for loopholes and give up early or even halfway through because you cannot find the energy and motivation to handle the changes. This chapter is dedicated to helping you overcome these negative thoughts and help you stay committed to the vegan cause:

Set yourself easy to achieve targets initially – Setting unachievable targets can put you off as you may then see yourself as a failure. Take a little at a time and be motivated by your small achievements. Slowly you will be able to set higher targets and achieve them too.

Keep a journal and food tracker and make diligent notes – Write down everything. From what to eat, how much you have exercised, how difficult the day was in terms of keeping you on track, what were the motivation factors, what were the de-motivation factors, and more! Make note of everything no matter how trivial it may seem. When you are looking back, these notes will come in handy and will help you correct any mistakes.

Interact with people who are also facing these challenges – We are social animals and love the sense of belonging and a sense of identity. When we reach out to people who face the same situations that we face, we find that sense of belonging and the fear that we are the only ones with problems goes away. Moreover, when we interact with other people, ideas and best practices can be exchanged which is good for all concerned.

Remember the process of change is always difficult and painful. But, if we do not take up these challenges we will stagnant which is the beginning of any end. You must steel yourself and work hard for a better tomorrow. When you are feeling low, think of the potential positive results of your endeavors and be motivated by those images and thoughts.

So, pick up the shovel, roll up your sleeves, take a firm stand, and start work immediately and rest assured that you will find happiness, contentment and an amazing sense of achievement at the end of this seemingly arduous journey.

You're fully committed- what's next?

You made it through your 30-day course! It took a lot of discipline and willpower, but you made it like a champion and are now feeling better than ever. Your energy is high, your mind is clear and you are ready to continue practicing a healthy vegan lifestyle! So, what's the next step? This section is here to give you a few kick-start ideas on how to keep up with the vegan diet and enhance the healthy new you even further.

Future Meal Planning

Maybe you want to go on with the vegan diet but aren't sure where to start, or the set meal plan was really what kept you going. If you enjoyed the recipes and plans in this book, you can go ahead and rotate the meals again! Many of the recipes are customizable with different selections and cover enough days with different types of treats that you won't grow tiresome. If you're adventurous and want to try your hand at creating your own meal plan, start with a simple online search. Blogs and websites are plentiful with great ideas and recipes- your favorite vegan meal may be out there waiting at the tips of your fingers on the keyboard! Then, if you are the extreme adventurist, creating your own recipes might just be a fun new hobby! Now that you are familiar with the common foods and structure of a healthy vegan meal, take some of your favorite elements and flavors and see what you can come up with. You may end up with a couple of hit or miss concoctions, but it will be worth the experience and the chance at creating something awesomely new!

Share the excitement

Did you go on this 30-day challenge alone and just can't keep the excitement of vegan living to yourself any longer? Tell people about it and how much better you feel eating and living healthy! Testimonies go a long way as inspiration for people who are feeling miserable in their current ways. You could even get a circle of friends interested in vegan lifestyle and start a newsletter or a blog to keep yourself involved while giving your group updates on new tasty recipes, tips, and motivation. Sometimes someone just needs a helping hand to get started, and your experience is just what they need! If no one you know seems too keen on the idea of vegan eating, or if you're not sure you have quite the knowledge and gusto to start up an info group of any sort, search online for a vegan-related forum or blog to follow yourself. You could earn support and knowledge while meeting new, like-minded people along the way. Win-win!

However, you decide to keep involved and fully invested in your new vegan lifestyle, just remember that that's what it is. A lifestyle that you chose for your health and your energy- an achievement to be proud of. Congratulations, and best regards!

Help me improve this book

While I have never met you, if you made it through this book I know that you are the kind of person that is wanting to get better and is willing to take on tough feedback to get to that point. You and I are cut from the same cloth in that respect. I am always looking to get better and I wish to not just improve myself, but also this book. If you have positive feedback, please take the time to leave a review. It will help other find this book and it can help change a life in the same way that it changed yours. If you have constructive feedback, please also leave a review. It will help me better understand what you, the reader, need to make significant improvements in your life. I will take your feedback and use it to improve this book so that it can become more powerful and beneficial to all those who encounter it.

REMEMBER TO JOIN THE GROUP NOW!

If you have not joined the Mastermind Self Development group yet, now is your time! You will receive videos and articles from top authorities in self development as well as a special group only offers on new books and training programs. There will also be a monthly member only draw that gives you a chance to win any book from your Kindle wish list!

If you sign up through this link http://www.mastermindselfdevelopment.com/specialreport you will also get a special free report on the Wheel of Life. This report will give you a visual look at your current life and then take you through a series of exercises that will help you plan what your perfect life looks like. The workbook does not end there; we then take you through a process to help you plan how to achieve that perfect life. The process is very powerful and has the potential to change your life forever. Join the group now and start to change your life! http://www.mastermindselfdevelopment.com/specialreport

21710744R00069

Printed in Poland
by Amazon Fulfillment
Poland Sp. z o.o., Wrocław